201 Great Story Ideas for Communicators

by Ed Bauer

Published by:

Ragan Communications, Inc.
212 West Superior St.
Chicago, IL 60610
312-335-0037

INTRODUCTION

Sometimes you need a story idea fast. On other days, you're at leisure to come up with an interesting idea: what you really want is insight into how to present that idea, or a new twist on an old theme. This book is for both occasions.

Maybe all you're seeking is a filler. Or else you're looking for a major story idea. What do you do when you know there's something you should be covering but you can't quite put your finger on it—and the angle to take?

This book is designed to fill all those needs—and more.

There have been big changes in organizational journalism in recent years. These days, communicators are not only allowed to cover the tough subjects—they are expected to. Not all of the coverage has been pretty. As you'll see in the pages that follow, at least one editor was trying to help his company battle back from Chapter 11. How would you like that assignment?

If you face challenges like these, you'll draw strength from the communicators who have gone before you. How have they handled shrunken budgets? Publications being eliminated or downgraded? Plant closings? Workers being asked to leave and never come back? You'll find out in this book.

You'll discover editors who help their readers cope with global competition. Other editors pinpoint who the national competition is and enlighten their readers about the strengths these competitors enjoy.

Some editors confront readers with the demands of the marketplace. Other communicators in multi-national firms grapple–successfully–with the difficulties of communicating across oceans. Leading publications, as you'll discover within these pages, go beyond reporting on their industry to help readers grasp how the world is changing.

If you read this book cover-to-cover, not only will you find many usable ideas but you'll come away with a better grasp of your job. You'll know how to handle just about any story. You'll spot stories you've somehow neglected. And you'll know the future holds many more opportunities for you. If you can't read the entire book, just browse whenever you need a good story idea!

—Ed Bauer

201 GREAT STORY IDEAS

Story Idea No. 1

**To get better response, ask:
Who made you what you are?**

Want a bigger reader response? Peter Vogt, managing editor of *Walgreen World,* had a great idea: Invite your people to tell the world about "one particular individual who made a difference in who you are today." Here's the twist: Begin the feature with a couple of provocative questions like Vogt did. He asked, "Would Plato have become a philosopher without his teacher Socrates? Would James Dean have been an actor if he hadn't seen Marlon Brando in 'On the Waterfront?'" Vogt awarded $10 for the best answers.

Story Idea No. 2

**An essay contest
Helps the environment**

Jack El-Hai, editor of Dayton Hudson's *Headlines*, asked employees to submit essays on the environment. He got his company to promise $1,000 to the local environment group of each winner's choice. El-Hai printed the essays of the four winners in *Headlines*.

Story Idea No. 3

**Ask how a phrase
Got into the language**

Editor Bob Hecker of Children's Hospital of Columbus, Ohio sent out a reporter on a hot summer's day to ask just one question of employees: What is the origin of the phrase "dog days" to describe the month of August? People came up with strange answers ("If a dog bites you in the 'dog days' it takes longer for the sore to heal"). Eventually the reader finds out that "dog days" refers to the period when Sirius, the dog star, rises with the sun. A good idea for the slow summer months.

Story Idea No. 4

Help the environment: Print carpool tips

Julie Griffith of Cedars-Sinai went to the hospital's rideshare coordinator, who gave readers of Griffith's *LifeLines* nine carpooling tips (e. g., "Arrange to meet potential driving partners before riding together to discuss carpool rules"). Jeanie Herbert of Beckman Instruments went one step further: She created a bimonthly newsletter devoted entirely to ridesharing. Her two-page *Commuter Clips* publicizes the Commuter Club, a plan that awards employees a $2 bonus plus special parking privileges every day they don't drive alone.

Story Idea No. 5

Find "heroes" of Customer service

Editor David Thomson of Continental Insurance offered $100 to any one of his readers who nominated an authentic "hero" of customer service. The "hero" gets a feature in the employee publication, *Currents*, and wider recognition in Continental's corporate advertising campaign, while the nominator gets $100. Employees can even nominate themselves.

Story Idea No. 6

"Editor's Helper" sticker
Gets many to contribute

Don Sanford, editor of Peabody's quarterly, *Pulse*, gives away sticker decals reading "Editor's Helper" to every employee who fills out the magazine's reply card. Even after two years of giving away decals, Sanford still gets about 100 cards a month from a reader base of about 15,000. The decals cost about 20 cents apiece.

Story Idea No. 7

Editor turns publication
into a comic book

Editor Jill Grever Sackett transformed *Onward*, her staid company publication, into a comic book and created a fictional "Secret Agent," a trench coat-clad insurance super salesperson for the Principal Financial Group. He moves from one real case history to another, showing how real-life agents have exhibited exceptional intelligence and foresight in meeting their customer's needs. She warns imitators to emphasize the serious theme and go easy on the cuteness.

Story Idea No. 8

Use back page teasers
To create reader interest

How do you get readers interested in what's coming up in your next issue? Rosemary Abrahams of Manulife Financial writes very short one-line teasers (e. g., "Is loyalty dead?") to describe articles in next month's issue, and places them on the back page of *Vista*, her monthly publication.

Story Idea No. 9

Create news brief section
For hard company news

Consider printing a half-page section of company news briefs, modeled after the *Wall Street Journal,* as John Hurst, editor of the *Alcan Ingot,* does. Written in a terse style, the hard news items are limited to about 250 words each, and are printed in unindented form with small italicized headlines.

Story Idea No. 10

**Motivate your readers
With employee tips**

Like every other editor, Wendy Conklin of Squibb prints pictures of employees in her magazine *ClearImage*. Unlike many other editors, Conklin then asks the pictured employees for motivational tips and suggestions on operations, customer service, and other company matters. Their very pointed, practical comments appear below their pictures in a feature called "Viewpoint."

Story Idea No. 11

**Write brief biographies
Of all new employees**

L. Marguerite Rho of Alexander & Baldwin, Inc., prints more than just the names and pictures of new employees in *Maui Today*. She also writes four-sentence capsule biographies detailing the person's job, division, education and previous experience. Also included: where the person lives and whether he or she is married. It's a good way of preventing a large organization from getting impersonal.

Story Idea No. 12

Employees serve as source
For little-known corporate facts

Sara Lee Corp.'s *Interchange* has a featurette entitled "Did you know?" that provides obscure (but interesting) facts about the company's many divisions. Editor Joanne Kitsos sends a bag of Sara Lee products to employee tipsters whose facts are published. This is a good way to get stories from outlying locations.

Story Idea No. 13

Ask the one question
That gets them going

Editor Carol Atlas of Aetna's *AetnaSphere* asked her readers to complete the sentence: "What this company needs is . . . ". She received many thoughtful responses to this query.

Story Idea No. 14

Tell them what your Competitors are doing

Editor Paula Kollstedt of GE Aircraft Engines writes a column called "Competition Watch" in her weekly newspaper *Headlines*. The column features short, timely items on rival firms. It's a good way of giving employees the bigger marketplace picture, and the feature is quite popular with readers. If someone in your company is keeping track of the competition, say through a clipping file, that's the person to cultivate for information. The sales department may be a good place to start your investigation.

Story Idea No. 15

Ask returning employees: Has the company changed?

B. C. Hydro has a new publication, *People*, the goal of which is to stimulate discussion by going out to employees and asking thoughtful questions. It then encourages employees to respond to what they've read. In a recent article, three workers who had left the company and then returned were asked whether the company had changed during their absence.

Story Idea No. 16

Chart company history
Through annual reports

The public relations department at Laclede Gas went back to a 1910 annual report to chart the company's history in their bi-monthly *The Laclede News*. They found that the report "contains only 12 small pages, has no pictures and prints negative financial numbers in red ink." While writing their company's story, they marked the evolution of the annual report into today's glossy marketing and recruiting tool, running photos of 15 annual report covers from the past.

Story Idea No. 17

Motivate employees
To stay healthy

Absenteeism can cripple any company's service. Nancy Johnsen, editor of the monthly *Watts & Drops*, is helping to eradicate absenteeism at the Lansing Board of Water & Light. The board has come up with a monthly lottery-style drawing in which workers with good attendance records can win from $25 to $1,000. Johnsen gives up a full page to report the lottery, jazzing up the story with good photos and catchy names for the prize categories.

Story Idea No. 18

Is your e-mail
A junk mail drop?

Sue Sell of Sears' *Tower News* did a story of "e-mail overdose," revealing that some colleagues got as many as 50 messages a day. She said "no one has time to wade through this flood every time they sign on." Her advice: Send more concise messages, and send FYI notices to the system's bulletin board rather than to other users' in-baskets.

Story Idea No. 19

Finally, a policy manual
That's always up-to-date

Joe Mark Horn, editor of Atmos' *Visions,* reported on an electronically produced company policy manual. One exec said "Having a manual on-line provides the user with the most current information. A paper document could be out of date before it reaches the manager's desk." The introduction of a company policy manual, or the revision of an existing manual, could make a good story. And if it's on-line, as this one was, the story gets even better.

Story Idea No. 20

For the environment: Give a "no-cup" option

Ask your company to install buttons on vending machines that allow drinkers to use their own mugs instead of paper cups. Sue Surendonk, editor of *The Daily*, a newsletter of the Aid Association for Lutherans, organized a contest among floors of her building to see which floor could use the fewest cups, and gave periodic updates on how each floor did. In one recent December, 12,000 cups were saved.

Story Idea No. 21

Off-beat features Fascinate readers

Two great regular feature ideas from editor Jay Dunner of the Philadelphia Reserve Bank: (1) review records, movies, or books. Dunner writes a pop music column in his publication. Readers love it. (2) a pot-pourri column of facts, statistics and tips on every conceivable subject, from every possible source. Dunner calls this feature "Just the Facts."

Story Idea No. 22

Prepare employees
To answer questions

Editor Mike Easterling of the Baptist Medical Center writes a column called "In Case You're Asked" in his publication *Team Works*. The column gives employees answers to questions likely to be raised by patients. One tip: Limit yourself to one question and answer per column. Some utilities use a variation of this theme. They consider their entire work force to be public relations representatives. Since utilities are constantly going before state commissions for rate increases, they provide pertinent facts about why the increase is needed on wallet-sized cards they distribute to employees. The workers refer to the cards when asked questions about the increase.

Story Idea No. 23

Time for your
30,000-mile PM?

Good health idea: Mary Gemignani of Mutual Life wrote a 17-point "program of preventive measures," and made it look like a car maintenance schedule. She advises readers as to how frequently they should check their blood pressure, cholesterol, and other indicators of health. It's a very useful clip-and-save item.

Story Idea No. 24

Use biographies
To present history

A fine feature story is lurking in your company's library, in its archives, or in the back files of your newsletter or magazine. Mary Story of Alabama Power did a powerful, moving reminiscence of a former chairman of that company who died in 1964 for her magazine *Powergrams*. Using biography to present history is a guaranteed way to spark and hold reader interest.

Story Idea No. 25

Spotlight employees'
Philanthropic work

Every year, editor Guy Davis of Frito-Lay puts out a short yearbook listing the hundreds of charitable projects that Frito-Lay employees have been involved with over the past twelve months. He binds this 16-page yearbook into the pages of the summer issue of his quarterly magazine. Davis divides the charities by theme—medical care, social welfare, the arts, etc.—and each section has a shaded column describing one project in depth. An impressive expression of company pride.

Story Idea No. 26

Turn your readers
Into a clipping service

Kris Fury buys magazine subscriptions for employees at Matthew Bender. The employees send her articles from other magazines that can be used in the monthly two-page supplement to *Inside Albany* entitled "Managing." This supplement goes to managers at the firm's three offices. She's turned her readership into a big clipping service, and we suspect that doing so enables her readers to work off—in a healthy way—frustrations with their managers. After all, the boss might read the article and get the hint.

Story Idea No. 27

The shocking facts
About "sidestream smoke"

When the Dartmouth-Hitchcock Medical Center's ban on smoking went into effect, Anne O'Connor, editor of *Center View*, wrote a short and shocking story. Instead of the usual "how to quit" piece, she came up with grim statistics about so-called "sidestream" cigarette smoke: secondhand smoke is actually dirtier than the stuff inhaled by the smoker; 50,000 Americans die each year of diseases connected with passive smoking. It's the strongest argument for a total ban on smoking in the workplace.

Story Idea No. 28

That mysterious other Holiday in December

Everything you wanted to know about Hanukkah, but were afraid to ask, editor Carol Saunders gave her readers in a short article about the Jewish holiday. It appeared in the weekly publication *Newsline*, issued by The Stamford Hospital. Run this one in your next end-of-the-year issue.

Story Idea No. 29

Ask employees to rate Company cafeteria

Finding out what employees think about the company cafeteria is a surefire idea. *Currents* editor Mary Gemignani asked employees to rate Mutual Benefit Life's cafeteria for the taste of its food, for service and cleanliness.

Story Idea No. 30

Reverse your company's Organization chart

Carolyn Zachary, editor of AT&T's *Focus*, re-drew the company's line chart as an inverted pyramid to show that "business units, where people are closest to the customer, are at the top of the organization." Putting tens of thousands of service reps at the top rather than bottom of the chart is a fine touch. It shows in graphic terms how AT&T is still oriented—even after divestiture—toward the outer world rather than toward the internal hierarchy. A great way of giving meaning to the "Customer Service is No. 1" platitude.

Story Idea No. 31

All-quotes newsletter Gets good free publicity

Editor/publicist Marsha Zabarsky of Beth Israel Hospital helps reporters in TV, radio and the newspapers get memorable quotes for their medical stories by writing a two page newsletter. It consists entirely of nuggets of medical wisdom from hospital authorities and doctors. These nuggets are ready to be pasted into a story and used as filler. Zabarsky gets her quotes from interviewing people, listening to lectures, and from casual conversation. She mails *Quote/Unquote* to about two hundred media people.

Story Idea No. 32

It's where you put
Your survey card

Jeanie Herbert gets bigger reader survey response by putting her survey card next to, and on top of, a trivia game that offers prizes to the winners. Herbert advises imitators to place the survey card away from the center staples, because readers are more likely to fill out what they have to tear out than what they can ignore. And if the card is near staples, it's much easier to rip out. Herbert edits *Beckman Life*, a publication of Beckman Instruments.

Story Idea No. 33

Remove fear to get
Reader letters

John Merlino of Southern Bell tried for three years to get letters from readers. After pleading, prodding, and printing any letters that trickled in, Merlino was finally rewarded: readers began writing him. Merlino publishes the critical and the controversial along with the pleasant. If your employees are like most, they fear retribution for speaking their mind. Merlino believes that through perseverance, by demonstrating over time there is no retribution, you can overcome this reluctance.

Story Idea No. 34

Publish an employee questionnaire, Then share the results with readers

If you see a dull news month coming up, create your own news. Barbara Reeve, of Universal Card Services Corp., did. She published a questionnaire that asked employees about job satisfaction, leadership, teamwork, and more. When your responses come rolling in—and they will if your survey can be answered anonymously as hers was—share the results with your readers as hard news.

Story Idea No. 35

Editor fills page with Valentine's Day feature

To secure input for a Valentine's Day feature, editor Teresa Gibson asked State Farm employees two questions in her January *Easterner:* How did you meet your spouse? How did your spouse propose to you? Responses were run in the next issue on a lacy, ornate page that resembled an old fashioned valentine.

Story Idea No. 36

Liven up those
Yearbook-like photos

If you're forced to run a lot of individual photos, such as those of persons who make up a committee, advisory board, etc., lighten things up. In addition to their photos, run their vital statistics, hobbies, and a quote giving each individual's secret of success, as the editor of Shearson Lehman Brothers' *Portfolio* did recently.

Story Idea No. 37

Run in their shoes—
Then picture it

Mary-Gordon Hagler, photographer for Riverside Methodist Hospitals, donned scrubs and followed a surgical nurse around during a recent 12-hour shift, taking photos on the run. When published in *Riverside Monthly,* the pictures revealed more eloquently than words alone the hectic pace these nurses endure. You might try a similar photo essay or particularly rigorous jobs your employees perform.

Story Idea No. 38

Retirees serve as
Feature material

It's fun to interview a lucid retiree who can tell your readers what the old days were like. As you can guess, such coverage is a hit with all retirees receiving your publication. Editor Gary Ortman found a 100-year-old woman who retired during the Eisenhower administration. She recalled the coming of the first autos, planes, and radios to central Illinois. Ortman highlighted her story in *Caterpillar Folks*.

Story Idea No. 39

Explaining corporate policies
Might minimize problems

Wisconsin Public Service Corp. editor Mary Pappas believes informed employees are less likely to get themselves or their employer in trouble. So she wrote an article in simple, non-threatening language on corporate policy in four key areas—sexual harassment, AIDS, drugs and alcohol, and safety. She asked readers of *Contact* to do some soul searching to discover if their attitudes were in accord with the spirit of these policies. If you suspect your company could encounter problems in key areas like these, why not spell out your firm's position? Do get clearance at high levels—certainly from your legal department—before you commit anything to print.

Story Idea No. 40

Suggestion award winners
May easily fill a page

Some companies have gung ho employees who make hundreds of suggestions. At other firms, the idea of suggestions excites no one. You'd have to have a large and active group of suggestion-givers to make what worked for *MTS Echo* editor Mike Daly work for you. Mike runs a full page of prize-winning employee suggestions every issue, providing recognition for contributors and awareness for his readership.

Story Idea No. 41

Who ya gonnna call?
Bureaucracy Busters!

A salute to Fran Aller Goldstein, who edits *Dateline International*. Every issue of this publication from American Express has a feature entitled "Bureaucracy Busters". The feature contains a reader-suggested way of opening up the corporation, as well as a response (usually sympathetic) from an executive. A feature every editor could emulate.

Story Idea No. 42

Level with readers
About future reductions

Hats off to *Pecten* editor Brian Burton and his employer, Shell Canada Ltd. The company leveled with employees, telling them in an unusually provocative headline, "Downsizing to continue well into decade." It prepared employees for the future and served as an example of what more and more workers are demanding of employers—honesty.

Story Idea No. 43

Clever nostalgia piece
Highlights CEO's anniversary

It was 1956 when the current CEO of Bob Evans Farms joined the company. *Homesteader* editor Tammy Roberts used the anniversary of the CEO's hiring to show, with a collage of facts (milk prices, top TV shows, etc.) and photos (of key execs then and now), just what 1956 was like. The idea works equally well for an important corporate anniversary, such as the completion of a new plant, the introduction of a new product, or a long-ago merger. Readers relish nostalgia pieces.

Story Idea No. 44

Add "to be given away" To your classifieds

If classified ads are a regular feature of your publication, consider adding a "to be given away" section. It's helpful to employees who are (1) cleaning the attic, (2) moving, or (3) seeking a new home for an unwanted pet. Thanks to editor Gary Quillen of *Eastman News* for the idea. Another idea: If certain items have been sold between the time you originally listed them and the time you actually go to press, put "SOLD" in boldface over those ads. This shows how effective your ad column is, and keeps people from wasting time in phone calls and visits.

Story Idea No. 45

Publish an index To your newsletter

To demonstrate that your publication has lasting importance, publish an annual index. That's what Diane Trach of Syncrude Canada's *Insight* newsletter does. The index appears in her January issue. She also makes it possible for readers to request back issues. If you don't want to use valuable editorial space for your index, provide it as an insert. And you might try to build enthusiasm for it by announcing its availability in the issue before it appears.

Story Idea No. 46

Get readers involved
With "claim to fame" contest

Editor Irene Cooper, in *Heartbeat*, publication of The Methodist Medical Center of Illinois, ran a returnable form which asked employees to list their claims to fame–longest commute, most states lived in, etc. The winners got prizes. This idea cuts across organizational lines and extends possible celebrity status to everyone. And because you're asking readers to take action, your contest may allow you to gauge your readership.

Story Idea No. 47

Make your service anniversaries
A potential news-creating event

Organize a no-holds-barred Q&A party to celebrate your company's next big anniversary. Editor Kathleen Housley of *Grumman World* sold management on turning part of a service anniversary meeting into a Q&A session with top officers, including the CEO. She printed the most relevant questions and responses. It's two-way communication that can build readership, assuming: (1) the questions are tough, and (2) the responses are brutally honest.

Story Idea No. 48

Here's a great idea
For your holiday issue

With help from the American Academy of Pediatrics (708-228-5005) editor Kathy Baugh came up with a list of ideas for Christmas toy shopping in the November issue of *Excelerator*. "You can make your shopping trip easier," she told readers. The information was supplied free by the Academy.

Story Idea No. 49

Provide realistic coverage
Of your disaster drills

A big photo of what appeared to be an accident victim, dripping with gore, seized the attention of editor Mitchell Nimmoor's readers. His monthly tabloid for hospital employees, *Nitty Gritty*, carried the headline "Disaster Strikes GHC" (Garden City Hospital). Nimmoor quickly explained that this was only a disaster drill, covered in greater detail inside. Since this idea involves a little trickery, you'll have to decide if it conforms to your editorial policy before using it.

Story Idea No. 50

Work late yourself
To cover night shift

If your organization has a night shift, most likely it isn't receiving the coverage day people get. Consider writing about your night shift workers even if it means staying late yourself. You'll find them friendly and willing to help out, as did *Visions* editor Joe Mark Horn. The angle he used–the loneliness of life on the graveyard shift–might work for you. His headline "Working with the Werewolves" grabbed reader attention.

Story Idea No. 51

Making videos interactive
Requires publication link

If you produce a news video, editor Jerri Etchason of *Seafirst News* has an idea to share. She features a trivia question and its answer in her quarterly news video. Viewers are then asked to write the answer on a coupon she runs later in her print publication. They send their answers to the communications department. Ten lucky entrants get cash prizes, and Etchason gets some idea as to how many employees are watching her video.

Story Idea No. 52

Featuring non-sexist jobs
Underscores lateral moves

Editor Amy Lawrence's photo essay in BellSouth Telecommunications' *Bama* shows that jobs aren't segregated by sex anymore. It looks at three nontraditional employees—a woman service technician, a woman cable splicer and a male service rep. Interestingly, each person moved sideways into his or her current job after starting in a more conventional position.

Story Idea No. 53

Boost family readership
With a lively kids page

Many editors say they want family readership, but unlike editor Ken Kane and his *BPA Circuit,* they do little to encourage it. Ken does. He runs an occasional "Kids Page," a poster-sized spread with an airy, child-friendly design. Ken's creations feature custom-drawn cartoons, large and easy-to-read type, and useful information. One recent sampling included such good information on the metric system it just might find its way into community schools.

Story Idea No. 54

Phone hotline secures
News tips from readers

Wisconsin Bell's *Trend Bulletin* edited by Lorna Sorenson features its own phone hotline. Why isn't everyone doing this? Actually, Sorenson offers readers a choice of three numbers—the corporate headquarters number, a location number, and an 800 number for workers outside Wisconsin. You might want to offer a small prize to anyone calling in news. This could reduce anonymous calls, as callers forsake anonymity for token gifts.

Story Idea No. 55

We're all numbers anyway,
Why not capitalize on this fact?

Find your employee number and win a prize. For her readers, it's as simple as checking a small back-page item in Lorraine Yorke's *To Everyone* publication. She runs four employee numbers each issue, then provides small prizes to readers who spot their numbers and call her. It's an inexpensive way to boost reader interest.

Story Idea No. 56

Pep up your publication
With a new colored stock

To give their publication new punch, the editors of the Navy's *Sealant* newspaper shifted from white to buff-colored paper. The added cost was very small. Colored stock can become a trademark for your publication. Be specific in selecting the stock and checking each issue until you're certain your printer has it right. Use the same stock, supplier, paper weight and finish each time. If you don't, issue savers will notice and your attempt at providing a quality appearance will backfire.

Story Idea No. 57

Your page numbering
Can reflect creativity

If you edit a publication read by creative people, follow the lead of Carole Lapensohn in *The Clipper*. She numbers her pages like this: Page 2wo; Page 3hree; Page 4our, etc., a kind of E.E. Cummings approach to what is normally a mundane chore.

Story Idea No. 58

Savvy corporate wives
Ease relocation blues

If you're a communicator for a multi-national firm, take a page from a group of Shell wives. They compiled a book of writings and drawings from families who have been moved all over the world. *Pecten* editor Margaret Sparkes reported on the anthology, which includes poems, anecdotes, travel advice, and cultural insights. You might suggest the idea to corporate spouses who have moved and who know how a book of tips could ease the stress of relocation. Corporate sponsorship could remove any financial risk for backers. Such a publication would be in a corporation's best interests anyway.

Story Idea No. 59

Putting top photo contest
Entries to good use

If your publication sponsors a photo contest here's how to put winning entries to good use: Display them in calendar form, as Pam Karg of the Dairyland Power Cooperative did. She also featured a snapshot of each winner, above a brief statement giving the circumstances surrounding the photo. Such a treatment provides ample display for all winning photos—something that isn't always possible if you cram them into a regular issue.

Story Idea No. 60

Good free-lance photos?
Here's how to get them

Even if your budget doesn't allow for a full time photographer, are you able to hire a free-lancer from time to time? If so, here's a tip from Mary Ellen Seitz, editor of SmithKline Beecham's *News*: scan your local newspaper to spot and hire the best free-lance photojournalists. When you give them their assignments, encourage them to snap away in natural light from as many angles as possible.

Story Idea No. 61

Far-ranging news
Draws readers in

Some editors feel constrained to cover their corporation like newspaper reporters cover the local scene. Other editors branch out. Jerri Etchason, editor of *SeaFirst News*, covers more than banking news. She writes about such disparate subjects as body language and the job market. You might try such an approach. General interest articles add spice and draw readers into the hard corporate news. Don't be afraid to pick up the phone and call some news maker. It may take some digging but it's worth it.

Story Idea No. 62

Get a retiree to write "How to write" column

Exxon Today carries a column on how to improve written communication. The unique twist: the lessons are drawn from actual company documents. Would management be willing to open its files to you? And do you have someone qualified to handle such a chore? Exxon relies on a retiree, Bill Hogan, to free-lance the items.

Story Idea No. 63

Honor employees who Accomplish the unusual

The customer isn't always right at KPL Gas Service—especially not when he or she tries to steal gas. Editor Marisa Daniels honored employees who discovered these energy thieves. She ran the employee names in *KPLife* in a feature entitled "Cut 'em off at the bypass." You can find an equally good way to pay tribute to your employees who go the extra mile.

Story Idea No. 64

If you want a gossip column, Don't try going it alone

No doubt gossip columns have high readership. But writing them every week isn't as easy as it looks. Besides being careful about libel, you must cultivate many sources. Rare is the individual who can do it alone. Seth Ellis, writer of a "Tell Me About It" feature in the St. Mary Medical Center *Messenger*, admits as much when he requests readers send him "good gossip on a timely issue" at the end of his first column.

Story Idea No. 65

Ask for interesting anecdotes On someone you plan to feature

In three months, you're going to cover the retirement of your CEO. To get outstanding material instead of the usual boring observations, share this open secret: ask your readers for reminiscences well in advance of the retirement. Editor James Hinkle asked readers to contribute anecdotes about the CEO in March, knowing the CEO would retire in May. You can use this idea with anyone who's retiring.

Story Idea No. 66

Celebrate your anniversary
By showing how far you've come

If your publication will celebrate a meaningful anniversary shortly, do what North York Hydro's *Charger* did—reprint your first issue as part of your anniversary issue. The older your publication is the more fun your readers will have. If it has undergone major changes in name or design, you might want to show the first examples of each. If possible, contact the original editor to get more color.

Story Idea No. 67

Need an editorial platform?
Consider the strategic plan

If your corporation has a strategic plan, that plan can provide an ideal editorial platform. All you've got to do is study the plan and think of stories that will help the company fulfill the plan. *Synergy* magazine (Wisconsin Electric) editor Robert Zahn says his eight-page monthly focuses on business issues and sticks to the strategic plan as a point of reference.

Story Idea No. 68

Explaining corporate benefits
Requires constant creativity

As employers shell out bigger and bigger benefit bucks they want employees to grasp all they're eligible for. Only when employees use their benefits do they understand them. That's why the employee benefit statement exists. State Farm editors Jim Bowers and Davina Coleman walk readers through the annual benefits statement, asking questions and providing answers. Their viewpoint? That of the typical employee, who's not exactly consumed with curiosity.

Story Idea No. 69

Promote cooperation
By publicizing appreciation

Airborne Express's *Today* grants a whole page to workers who wish to thank each other. Each of the 13 letters in a recent "Peer-To-Peer" column began with the recognized employee's name printed in conspicuous red ink and the letter writer's in bold black. Letters range from rave reviews ("It's people like you every manager dreams about") to graceful compliments ("Thanks for all your help").

Story Idea No. 70

Recapture the glow
Of long-ago columns

The chairman of Empire Southwest published a book containing more than 30 years worth of his "Chairman's Messages". Several thousand copies were printed; employees could request free copies from the communication department. Editor Terry Ertter, impressed by the chairman's "incredibly prophetic" grasp of today's problems, printed excerpts from his book in the company newsletter *Inside Track*. But you don't need to put together a book to capture the wisdom of ancient columns. Simply visit your archives and select some you like. Run them when your current columnist is on vacation.

Story Idea No. 71

Editor's tools
For April Fool's

By including a form for employees to fill out in her February issue, Fleet/Norstar's Therese Myers, editor of *New Directions*, was loaded for bear when it came time to write about what transpired on April 1. She collected stories of the clever pranks pulled on employees. It's an idea that can work for you as long as: (1) you're not blamed for promoting pranks, and (2) they don't become too outlandish.

Story Idea No. 72

Q&A approach ideal treatment
For covering a reorganization

Don't underestimate the value of a Q&A approach, especially if your story is lengthy and detailed. Editor Gay Lynne Stockwell-Rouse used Q&A to cover a reorganization at Tenneco Gas in the employee magazine *On the Line* Your Q&A must ask the questions typical readers would ask. Each reader can select exactly the information he or she wants. Q&A offers instant communication, speed reading instead of one column of type after another.

Story Idea No. 73

New hotline responds to
Communications questions

When Ameritech Services employees call the company's Information Hotline phone mail system, they get information on the communication department's programs—when the next TV broadcast will be, or where editor Judith Myer's *Bulletin* is distributed. Calls are monitored daily and the staff promises to reply to all questions within two days. That's the way to make communications more responsive.

Story Idea No. 74

Missing cartoon caption
Spurs reader action

To create reader interest and response, do what *Spirit* editor Robb Zerr did. He printed a captionless cartoon and asked readers to submit captions. He ran the responses the following month, offering a prize for the best.

Story Idea No. 75

Answering questions
Is your job as editor

Addressing the Manitoba chapter of IABC, editorial director Carolyn Zachary of AT&T told her audience that employees have four basic questions: (1) Where is the company going? (2) How will it get there? (3) How is it doing? (4) Where do I fit in? Answer these questions in your publication and you'll have done your job well.

Story Idea No. 76

Profile forgotten persons: Corporate directors

Editor Charles Belbin led off one of his recent issues of *Compass*, from Alcan, with a story titled "The Buck Stops Here." Included were mini-biographies of the 14 members of the board of directors, along with a brief account of their activities and duties. For the cover, Belbin selected a photo of the imposing table around which the directors assemble. Corporate boards are usually forgotten people. Letting employees know who is on the board makes for interesting reading.

Story Idea No. 77

It's great public relations To recognize volunteers

Cargill Inc. honors employees and retirees who serve as volunteers in their communities with a Volunteer's Recognition Day. Editor Paul Dienhart wrote a piece that publicized the good deeds of Cargill's people. Volunteer day stories are outstanding public relations and have the potential of being picked up by the media. Spend extra time talking to the voluteers, getting anecdotes about their experience as volunteers. Ask them how they came to volunteer. It's worth it.

Story Idea No. 78

Quote the CEO
Next to Joe Doakes

"What makes a good employee?" Editor Shanda Crosby printed the answer of the president of the East Kentucky Power Coop right next to the answers of John and Jane Doe, line workers, and turned a routine feature story into a memorable one. While the line workers stressed such traditional virtues as punctuality and loyalty, the president wanted line workers to better understand the big picture. The contrast between the comments made the column must reading. Remember this trick when you're disappointed with the quotes you've gathered on a topic.

Story Idea No. 79

When passing out credit,
Solicit all the help you can

When it comes to credit, everyone wants it. Editor Rhonda Smith obliges in the "Doin' it Right!" section of her Jackson National Life publication, *New Times*. She solicits nominations from every department and regional office. Judging from the dozens of names she mentions each month, employees have bought into this outstanding recognition program. Such a section provides positive reinforcement for your readers, and helps to tie everyone together if your company has numerous offices and plants.

Story Idea No. 80

To find interesting employees
Ask for help from readers

Readers are assets to be tapped. When American Can's *ANC People*, a special publication devoted to employees' off-the-job stories, was begun, readers were asked to submit nominations of interesting workers. Forty-two employees were covered in the publication, winnowed from 80 nominations. The publication served as a completely people-focused employee annual report. When you don't know how to bring off a particularly good idea for a story, ask your readers for help.

Story Idea No. 81

When your company goes international,
Start singing from the same song book

When Square D, a Chicago-area manufacturer of electrical equipment, was purchased by a French conglomerate, *Connections* editor Ellen Hake adapted to the change by initiating a series of "Cultural Exchange" columns. They show how employees sent overseas have adapted to the different business styles and manners they've encountered. Her features often quote foreigners on how they perceive American business and working methods. Savvy editors make certain their publications help everyone adjust to change.

Story Idea No. 82

Celebrate Earth Day
With special contest

SB News editor Mary Ellen Seitz includes a small coupon in the March issue of her publication. It's for readers to provide environmental tips. Winners got their tips printed in the April issue to observe Earth Day and received a gift. SmithKline Beecham sponsors the contest to get ideas "that will make the earth a cleaner place." You might structure your contest so that only people who come up with ideas which can immediately be put into action are winners.

Story Idea No. 83

Consider doing a quarterly
Just about company stats

The Quarterly, a new publication launched by Aid Association for Lutherans (AAL), has one mission: Show how the company has done, and how results will affect pay. AAL links pay to corporate and individual performance, so employees have a vital interest in keeping up to date on the latest sales figures. Besides quarterly statistics, the newsletter has a message from the president and goals for the coming quarter. Information is presented in reader-friendly charts and graphs. Editor Cheryl Coots says that making the connection between results and pay is essential, and the facts prove she's right. Second-quarter and third-quarter results were the best in corporate history.

Story Idea No. 84

Tips on communicating
With a global audience

It isn't easy to communicate with a global audience, says *Bank World* editor Thierry Sagnier. He suggests: (1) Use simple English. Since it is the second most complex language after Chinese, there's no point in making it more complicated. (2) Machine Assisted Translation (MAT). Use at your own risk. It's cheap but not always accurate. "MAT once translated the name of our former president (Barber Conable) into French as 'Hairdresser Conable'." (3) Translation consulting firms. Better than MAT, but costly. Typesetting in a foreign alphabet is also quite expensive. Another publication, Amex's *Dateline International*, provides translated summaries of important articles in French, Spanish and Japanese. Editor Fran Goldstein uses a consulting firm for translations since it offers excellent quality. Goldstein's translated feature accounts for the biggest percentage of the publication's budget.

Story Idea No. 85

Develop a newsletter
For contributing editors

Just what you need—another publication! But if you've got a staff of contributing editors reporting to you, a small newsletter might be in order to remind them of deadlines, pass out congratulations, offer hints on grammar, communication issues, writing and design, dealing with bosses, and so forth. Fleet Financial Group's *New Directions* editor Therese Myers began putting out *STET & dele* on the side because it provided an excuse to learn desktop publishing. It creates a feeling of togetherness for her contributing editors. It also affords her the chance to shed the organizational tone. Once your new publication is up and running, do a feature on it in your other publication(s).

Story Idea No. 86

Helping employees decide
Best way to communicate

When do you fax? When should you send a package overnight? When should you call? Internal and external communications can be costly: Employees use eight major communication methods, observed Wausau Insurance's *Good People* editor Pamela Henkel. She created a chart for readers that showed the various communication modes as well as covered such factors as time, message content, length, and cost. It was a helpful, money-saving device that savvy employees clipped and saved.

Story Idea No. 87

The editor unmuzzle, Make a crossword puzzle

Crossword puzzles involve readers like few other features can. *Noon Extract,* a two-pager from Merck, recently featured a crossword puzzle testing readers' knowledge of stories in earlier issues. Employees submitted completed puzzles; six winners received free lunch. Editor Karen Mehlbaum ran the answers in a subsequent issue. If making crossword puzzles simply isn't your cup of tea, get help from your art department, or find a free-lance artist. Editor Stanley Whitehead includes crossword puzzles on the back page of his *Cubelet Press.* "Across" clues refer to general knowledge; "down" clues are based on his newletter's articles.

Story Idea No. 88

Glossaries define jargon Employees must grasp

When American Express embarked on a new quality program it quickly became evident that there were a lot of new terms which weren't understood—more than 100 in all. The group in charge of the company's quality initiative issued a "Quality Leadership Glossary." If your company is going down the same path, offer the pages of your publication for such a glossary.

Story Idea No. 89

Help workers help themselves
To improved writing skills

Scanner editor Shannon Kelly, with the Hennepin County Medical Center, prints a regular feature on better writing. A staff writer assembles the column, which focuses on developing a clear, simple style. The column ends by asking readers what tricks they know to help them remember spelling, punctuation, or usage—making this truly an interactive writing feature.

Story Idea No. 90

Poems, inspirational quotes
Fill formerly blank back covers

Northwest Banker editor Chris Moore puts a short poem or inspirational quote on the back cover of her publication. It gives some personality to the issue and ends it on a reflective note. This is an excellent way to prevent too much white space on the back page.

Story Idea No. 91

Front page teasers
Liven up publications

"What's special about these numbers: 70,000/2,175? /see pages 5 and 6." "Count those jellybeans/Page 11." More tantalizing than a dry list of regular features, followed by page numbers, these little headlines from the *NB Tel News* quickly draw readers inside. They're on the front page where they can't be missed.

Story Idea No. 92

A Thanksgiving classic garners
Highly personal revelations

In the November issue of *Powergrams*, photo editor Bill Snow asked half a dozen employees "What are you most thankful for?" The honest and thoughtful responses made the feature, which was enhanced by running the answers under good-sized photos. This idea doesn't hit the top of the charts for creativity—but it does work.

Story Idea No. 93

Just because you can't cover it
Is no excuse for ignoring it

When *U. S. West Today* editors Lisa Best and Don Johnson couldn't cover some late-breaking national political news important to their company, they explained to employees why they couldn't write the story—a bill was slowly making its way through Congress. They covered the outcome in their next issue. Just because you can't alert readers to the outcome of a story doesn't mean you shouldn't let them know something is afoot.

Story Idea No. 94

Print updated employee
Addresses at Christmas

Eileen Scholes, who edits the *Central Hudson Newsletter*, knows employees and retirees like to exchange Christmas cards. Because employees often lose track of each other, Scholes prints updated addresses every November. However, check with top management first. Not too long ago many corporations wouldn't release this information for fear it would get in the hands of union organizers. There's also the privacy issue. You might request all employees who wish to be included to drop your publication a note.

Story Idea No. 95

Sponsoring a slogan contest
Delivers a message to all

W. Edwards Deming, the guru of total quality, doesn't like quality slogans. But what if the motto in question comes from an employee? Perhaps even Deming would relent. When Timken Co. held a slogan contest, the judges received close to 500 entries. The winning entry, as printed in the *Exchange*: "Quality: you demand it as a customer. Take pride in it as a supplier." Employee Kevin Kelly won $100 for his effort.

Story Idea No. 96

Every employee survey
Demands follow-up

Without follow-through an employee survey is useless. Pam Schroeder, editor of *St. John Today*, knows how important quick follow-up is. When she knew she couldn't provide results fast, she kept employees informed: "Employee Opinion Survey progress: Slow but sincere." Schroeder was bringing readers up-to-date about a survey from the previous year. The sooner you announce results, the more credibility you have. Share some of the results as soon as possible; employee cooperation will be better next time. If the survey resulted in better cafeteria food, that makes an even better story.

Story Idea No. 97

Your newsletter is
A corporate nerve center

A newsletter is a corporate clearinghouse, yet too few editors exploit this role. An exception is Barbara Donato, editor of *ChangeMaker!*, who asked readers at different plants to share ideas on environmental initiatives. When employees provided the information, Donato printed the ideas in a subsequent edition. Any key issue is fair game for this approach.

Story Idea No. 98

"I heard it through
The grapevine"

Everyone is "qualitied" to death these days, so it's up to editors to find new ways to tell the same story. Pay attention to the company grapevine. It could provide you with a unique twist. Recently at Garrett Fluid Systems Division, Maureen Rojas, editor of *Keeping in Touch*, chronicled a factory work group that chose its own supervisor. She quoted the skeptical members of the group; sidebars gave the employees' and management's opinions on the selection process. Stories like this often wind up in the local or trade press—deservedly so.

Story Idea No. 99

Why not feature Employee pets?

Editor Lauraine Perry, in a regular one-column item called "Extendi-Pet," in Perry's *Next* magazine, profiles the furry and feathered companions of Extendicare employees. Is it cutesy? Maybe, but it works in her publication. Her readers work for a nursing home chain, where pet therapy for patients is popular.

Story Idea No. 100

Corporate glass ceiling Draws blunt coverage

In an unusually frank story, Upjohn's *Intercom* admits that obstacles block the progress of women executives and that the turnover rate for women is twice as high as for men in equivalent positions—"and we don't know why." Managing editor Richard Chambers is to be commended for tackling this thorny topic.

Story Idea No. 101

When you're going under, Come up with something

StraightTalk is simplicity itself. This monthly two-pager from the Circle K food store chain contains only two features: A letter signed by the company's CEO and COO, and a two-column Q&A, packed with no-nonsense answers to tough employee questions. Text-heavy and dry in tone, *Straight Talk* is not a fun read. Yet employees like it because of its two cardinal virtues—candor and interaction. The publication is the offspring of Circle K's bankruptcy. Another, less solemn publication—*Counter Talk*—handles normal employee communication. If your company is in a slump, maybe a new publication is in order.

Story Idea No. 102

Ask readers To criticize

MHHD Magazine editor Maria Martino asked readers to critique a recent issue and also to submit story suggestions. In return for their help, Martino provides participants with a couple of booklets, one on communication tips, another on health. She also encourages readers to fax their late-breaking news items to her.

Story Idea No. 103

Bringing government regulation
Into the homes, hearts of readers

If unfavorable legislation or regulation threatens your industry, you can get readers on your side. Some of them will write protest letters to Congress. *United Spirit* editor Dale Merkel wrote a strong anti-regulation story: "WARNING: This newspaper contains one or more toxic chemical substances known to cause cancer, birth defects, or other reproductive harm." He told employees that a state initiative would require facilities that store any of 458 listed chemicals to mail twice-yearly warnings to all nearby residents. It would also require an extensive system of worksite labeling. His lead sentence makes the point that dangerous substances are in universal use every day. Good journalism, good politicking.

Story Idea No. 104

If you run CEO letters,
Do it with style

Chemsphere editor Lawrence Basapa knows how to format the CEO's missive for maximum effect. His "President's Podium" has an actual headline, there's a name under the photo, and the letter is strong on substance. It avoids the usual platitudes. The rubric, photo, and name are placed to the side, suggesting that it's the individual's message, not his status, that counts.

Story Idea No. 105

Identify and discuss
Your corporate culture

The CEO of Ameritech recently told employees: "We are nice people. There aren't many people who have grown up in our business with the killer instinct...We've got to argue with each other more and accept each other on the basis of argument, whether we win or lose. We've just got to unleash the talent to be successful in our markets." For over 100 years Bell Telephone didn't have to compete, and its CEO was painting a picture of a corporate culture turned a little complacent. Perhaps you could get your CEO to do the same thing, especially if your company must undergo far-reaching changes.

Story Idea No. 106

Do a reality check
On new services

When you think of people to interview for your publication, do you ever consider your customers? If you've been offering new services, ask if the new approach is welcomed or is a pain in the neck. Editor Bob Bossert of US West Today's *Business & Government Services* recently wrote a feature highlighting one of his firm's top corporate clients. The focus of the article: what the client thought of a new service offered by US West.

Story Idea No. 107

Watch the vice-president
Drive a garbage truck

Editor Vivian Pearson had a field day, literally, when she wrote about the one day a year when higher-ups of Waste Management of North America work alongside line people. She also got some great photos. Just picture the human resources "biggie" run a forklift; watch as the CEO does a dispatcher's work. Get your company to sponsor a day like this and the photo ops and quotes may never end. Pearson's *WMI Report* made everyone look good.

Story Idea No. 108

Find a local angle
To a national story

It's so basic many of us forget it—find a way to tie your employer to a national story. Editor Shannon Kelly discussed the fact that Hennepin County Medical Center didn't encounter many medical emergencies when Minneapolis hosted the Super Bowl. Her headline in the *Scanner* told it all: "Super Bowl XXVI: It came, it went, we yawned." The hospital staff—while primed for any emergency—was able to take it easy during the game. Can you find local angles to national news stories? If so, you'll have a lot of fun.

Story Idea No. 109

**Don't avoid
The results of
Drug testing**

Editor Marilyn Matula, in her *Donnelly News*, released the good news about the first round of drug testing at Donnelley. Five percent of all randomly chosen employees tested positive—well below the national average. She revealed both the total numbers and the kinds of drugs ingested. Two-thirds of the offenders tested positive for marijuana. Less than two percent were shown to have traces of dangerous drugs in their systems.

Story Idea No. 110

**Reassure employees quickly
In tough economic times**

If management goes on record with reassuring words when employees suspect the worst, report this news immediately. Editor Marty Kusel was smart to run in *The Paper* a message addressed to EG&G employees by a company manager who underscored the importance of quick communication during tough times: "One thing is certain: Communicating with our employees is important . . . I pledge to you that we will communicate with you whenever we can as soon as we can."

Story Idea No. 111

Personal safety tips
Make good reading

Many publications swarm with health hints, most commonly doling out diet advice. Personal safety gets too little attention. Editor Pam Schroeder corrected this situation in her *St. John Today* by providing useful tips such as walking "with an air of authority and purpose when moving back and forth between your car and your ultimate destination." She points out that confident people "are less likely to be chosen as victims."

Story Idea No. 112

Take the mystery
Out of politics

Communications specialist Anne Sonnee got an employee committee to write a story on political primaries for her. The committee was promoting political participation at Fortis Benefits Insurance. The committee explained in *Employee Express Extra!* how to distinguish an open, indirect primary from a closed, direct one. The article explained political caucuses as well. Stories about politics play especially well around election time.

Story Idea No. 113

Profile a corporate building
Instead of an employee

Tired of profiling employees? Write up a company building instead. *Boeing Helicopter News* recently featured the oldest building on their corporate campus—Building 3-50. The building is an art deco office tower built in the late 20s. Otis Reed's article touched on the building's quirks, such as an interior balcony that allowed managers to address assembled workers from on high. The fact that the tower was slated for demolition added to the poignancy of this piece.

Story Idea No. 114

Try direct approach
To secure feedback

Inside AGCS isn't subtle in its request for feedback. The reply card for its "Inside Line" upward communication feature bears this plea: 'TALK TO US!" Who wouldn't respond to such a heart-felt plea?

Story Idea No. 115

Be not afraid to ask
The absurd question

Have some fun with your readers once in awhile. Ask for the silly, the absurd, the outrageous. Editor Ted McInnis, in his employee magazine for the Nova Scotia Liquor Commission, *The Spirited Informer*, asked employees to send him "the corniest country-and-western song title (real or made up)." He received some great submissions. Your readers could be just waiting for you to ask a question like this.

Story Idea No. 116

Sell your readership survey:
Appeal to their self-interest

If you're not getting the response you'd like to your readership surveys, perhaps you're not writing great "sell copy" when you introduce them. *Connection* editor Tom Geddie constantly polls readers, and introduces his survey with this statement: "The time [is] well spent as a source of story ideas, as a 'road map' for setting objectives and keeping them on target...and as one means of increasing employee involvement in decisions." Tell readers what's in it for them.

Story Idea No. 117

Success is in the eyes
Of the beholder

Gulf Power Co. President D. L. McCrary told readers of *Gulf View* that the company's greatest success of the year had been in improved communications. While his comments were interesting, the story could have been improved by asking workers at various levels what they thought the greatest success of the firm had been. The contrasting views would have made a good story better.

Story Idea No. 118

Your lobbyist is
An interesting story

The *MB Journal*, publication of MacMillan Bloedel Ltd., profiled a veteran government relations VP who was about to retire. The subject described his activities in the corridors of power as "creative loitering." His secret: he talked to people as often as he could and as informally as possible. Don't wait until your corporate lobbyist is retiring to write about this individual.

Story Idea No. 119

Use typography to unveil
A hidden quotation

When Cigna celebrated its 200th birthday *Cigna News* editor Gene Morris initiated a year-long contest. Every issue contained a word or words printed in a fancy 18th-century typeface. Unscrambled, the words formed a relevant quotation. Readers who correctly deciphered the message could enter their names in a prize drawing. An excellent way to get employees to scan entire issues, time after time.

Story Idea No. 120

You heard it wrong
Through the grapevine

Continental Airlines uses e-mail to report back to employees about rumors. Employees transmit the latest tidbit to the communications staff, which does some research and reports the facts of the situation. The staff goes as high as necessary to nail down the truth or falsehood of the rumor. Even the silliest rumors are taken seriously. Why? "There is a minority of employees who will believe the worst no matter what we say," observes employee communications director Ray Scippa. You, too, can combat harmful rumors in your publication.

Story Idea No. 121

Observe M. L. King Day
With diversity article

Excel devotes its Martin Luther King Day issue to the topic of workforce diversity at Minnesota Mutual. Editor Peter Stathopoulos accomplished a lot in his brief four-page format. The centerpiece was a series of statements by both black and white employees on what King meant to them. The editor also publicized what Minnesota Mutual is doing about diversity, and suggested sensitivity-training for readers.

Story Idea No. 122

Compare your company
To your competitors

Financial results become more meaningful when placed in perspective. One tried and true way has always been to compare this year's fourth quarter with last year's. *Continental Currency* editor Debby Storms makes her numbers more meaningful by comparing them to the results at ten of Continental Bank's peer institutions.

Story Idea No. 123

Create a special issue—
The "Year in Review"

Martin Marietta Energy Systems printed an encyclopedic "Year in Review" issue. The 10 by 12 inch magtab fits an amazing amount of information in its eight pages—perhaps too much—but that's forgivable in a publication meant for long-term reference. It featured bylined department reports—a good way to get writing help—and used gray bars to set items apart.

Story Idea No. 124

Publicize ways
To save money

Refill toner cartridges. Turn office machines off when not in use. Use scrap paper for note taking. Printing a story full of money-saving tips usually endears an internal communicator to senior management. The editor of *Flame,* from Cascade Natural Gas, took this approach recently and with good results. While the advice was rudimentary it was also useful.

Story Idea No. 125

Save your readers' time
By providing summaries

Continental Bank's publication, *Continental Currency*, is quick to scan, thanks to editor Debby Storms' use of brief marginal notes throughout the publication. The bold-face notes summarize stories, provide supplementary information, and act as quick announcements. The publication is a tabloid.

Story Idea No. 126

End every issue
With a brief test

Here's a quick way of letting readers know whether they've done full justice to your publication: Simply end each issue with a short quiz. Editor Jim Spangler of *Amoco Torch* prints his readership quiz on his back page. At the bottom of the back page he lists the answers and the page on which they're found; he even includes a score card.

Story Idea No. 127

Forget the position paper: Make it a memo to Hillary

Shannon Kelly's *Scanner,* a publication of the Hennepin County Medical Center, begins with a full-page "memo to Hillary Clinton" on the role of community hospitals. Monette Johnson, the director of public relations, uses the letter form to point out the hidden costs in maintaining an inner-city trauma center. It's much more readable than a boring, predictable reproduction of the standard position paper.

Story Idea No. 128

Allow your supervisors To thank their people

Julia Carey, editor of *Imprint*, asked managers at Meredith Publishing to tell her readers about the "stars" in their support staffs. Carey received a good number of letters from supervisors more than ready to publicly thank their employees. Put this idea in your perennial story ideas file—you can't run too many acknowledgement articles.

Story Idea 129

Keep investors informed;
Publish a stock update

When the editor of Pacific Press's *Newsline* started publishing a stock update for employees who had invested in the firm, she got mixed reviews from readers. Editor Linda Muller said that the vast majority applauded the update. However, one letter noted "The stock update in *Newsline* is a bad idea. Many of us bought our shares at $33! [At the time the letter was received, the stock stood at $19.] The update reminds us how much money we've lost." This idea gains in value if the stock in your corporation isn't listed in the newspapers your readers see.

Story Idea No. 130

Should you begin
An advice column?

The tabloid *Kmart Merchants* features a new item. Editor Michele Paulson developed an advice column called "Dear Carol Anne" and it uses the Ann Landers touch to discuss discount retailing problems. If you've got a large, scattered readership, it's possible you could garner enough letters to sustain such a column. Or use the column only when you've accumulated enough material.

Story Idea No. 131

Walk around to
Gather stories

"I try to find time once a week to walk around an hour or two in different company facilities," says Dick Henderson, editor of Union Carbide's *Carbider*. The weekly regimen helps employees get to know him; it also serves as a source of story ideas. Henderson has been doing it for 40 years, and just about every employee in the big West Virginia plant knows him by sight. "It's a good way to build rapport with readers," says Henderson. "They're pleased to see someone gathering news—rather than sitting behind a desk."

Story Idea No. 132

Discuss competitors
Of your organization

If your company is facing tough competition these days, own up to it. Run a story that gives succinct accounts of major rivals—their histories, emphases, and strengths. Colleen Niccum of Hughes Aircraft Missile Systems Group asked a company analyst to write a story about Hughes' competitors. Niccum ended her story with this quote from Chinese philosopher Sun Tzu: "Those who know not only themselves, but also their enemy, will be victorious."

Story Idea No. 133

Corporate communications
Could be a good feature

Make employees aware of your organization's communications abilities. You'll increase the likelihood that they'll use them. Editor Christine Jensen promoted this awareness on the first two pages of *Mayo Today*. By glancing through summaries of the medical center's telecommunications, video teleconferencing, computer networking, and nurse exchange programs, employees learned in three minutes what it's taken the Mayo Clinic years to implement.

Story Idea No. 134

Article helps employees
Handle difficult co-workers

Editor John Gerstner had fun with a recent article he ran in *JD Journal*, a publication of Deere & Company. He listed ten personality types that can give co-workers fits. He told readers how to spot these individuals and how to either win them over or neutralize them. Leading the list was the procrastinator: "Attracted to water fountains and coffee machines, he's consumed more liquids than all participants in Operation Desert Storm." Advice: "He's using you to help himself procrastinate. Ask him what he's been doing lately." Ten expressive faces illustrated the story and helped to flesh out the personalities.

Story Idea No. 135

Don't forget motor pool
For moving stories

If your employer provides a pool of cars for business travel, interview the head of the motor pool. You can learn a lot—and so can your readers—about vehicle maintenance, unusual accidents, etc. Washington Water Power recently added two bicycles to their car pool. *Weekly* editor Dana Williams sold the low-tech transport scheme to employees. She developed a chart that showed that 2-3 mile trips take no more time on a bicycle than in a car.

Story Idea No. 136

React quickly to a crisis;
Keep employees informed

Los Angeles corporate editors reacted quickly to the South Central riots of 1992. *World Currents* editor Karen Honeycutt issued a special edition when a World Savings branch office was destroyed. One issue of her quarterly was at the printer, and the next issue wouldn't appear for several months. So she wrote her story about the burned office, and printed it in a plain two-page format. Attached to it was a letter from a manager commending employees on their quick recovery from the disaster. When disaster hits it's no time to hide in the trenches. Just like war correspondents, you're expected to be on the front line.

Story Idea No. 137

Corporate milestones are
Good contest material

If your organization is on its way to an important milestone, sponsor a contest in which employees guess either the date and time, or figures connected with the milestone. This can be fun and enlightening. *Gulf Currents* recently sponsored a "Guess the Peak" Contest. Employees, after consulting almanacs and ouija boards, predicted when the highest power demand would occur. Winners received appropriate prizes—surge protectors. This idea is adaptable to many other situations.

Story Idea No. 138

Introduce new products
With an employee discount

If your employer produces and markets consumer products, see if you can't offer your readers a "cents-off" coupon. Georgia Pacific employees found a coupon in a recent issue of *Growth* allowing them 15 cents off the company's latest product—bathroom tissue for kids. Plan it so your coupon appears in the middle or at the end of your story about the introduction of a new product.

Story Idea No. 139

Employees as teachers: An interesting topic

Federal-Mogul's *World* covered an interesting twist on the empowerment movement—employee self-education. One of their plants' employee involvement councils created a seminar on manufacturing processes, led by workers with specialized knowledge of the various subjects. Any time you recognize employees who are teaching others it makes a good story.

Story Idea No. 140

Bulletin board feature Practically writes itself

The "Briefly" section in *Highlights* differs from many announcement pages because it's completely open to employee messages. To get a tidbit printed, all USAA employees have to do is send a note to the communications department explaining the who, what, when and where, and specifying publication dates. Some "Briefly" subjects: Discount tickets, sports scores, credit union offerings, bank-sponsored classes, and high school reunions. The format puts the responsibility for reporting employee events where it should be—on employees.

Story Idea No. 141

Tell your employees about
TV ads, program sponsorships

Subaru Spirit editor Debbie Weinstein lists the TV programs that carry Subaru commercials so that readers can keep up with the latest advertising. This makes advertising dollars go further, since employees will tell friends and neighbors when their company is sponsoring an important program or event. If your organization spends big on TV ads and program sponsorship, let your people know. Often, with help from your advertising department, you can get photos promoting sponsored programs . . . and you can publicize celebrities who will either be appearing or doing the announcing.

Story Idea No. 142

An employee romance
Makes a nice feature

Tim and Kelly Blanchard found romance at the check-out counter at Raley's Superstores grocery chain. He was a checker, she a courtesy clerk. "We just bagged each other," said Kelly. That was 11 years and two children ago. Editor Carl Bray wrote this delightful feature in *Superstories*. Ask around. You'll probably discover some interesting romances in your company.

Story Idea No. 143

Let locals know who
Butters their bread

You've got a winner when employees start grabbing your publication as soon as you put it in the rack. That's what happened to editor Ryndee Carney with a recent issue of his *Direct Connection*, a publication of GM's Packard Electric. The reason? The publication carried a page of coupons, each printed with this message: "Because I am an employee of Packard Electric Division of General Motors I am paying this bill with income from that job. I live in, work in, pay taxes in, and support a variety of businesses like yours in my community. I help support you, your job, and your business. I hope that when you choose to buy an automobile you will remember this and hopefully support my job and my organization by purchasing a General Motors product. Thank you." Employees clipped the coupon and put it in the envelope whenever they paid a bill.

Story Idea No. 144

Remove the mystery
Of upward advancement

Bonnie Benz, a communicator at Gulf Power, raised THE question in her *Gulf View*. What's the question? "How do employees get a promotion?" Simple, right? And if done well, guaranteed to have high readership. So why do so few internal publications ask it?

Story Idea No. 145

If sacrifice is needed
Find a way to show it

In hard times companies pull in their horns. Sometimes companies suffer from a double whammy—times are tough and the outlook in their particular industry is grim. One example: the airlines industry. Ray Scippa, associated with *CO Times*, says that bad times have pushed communications at the bankrupt Continental Airlines away from sugar-coating and toward the hard nut of truth. In one issue he attacked American Airlines for cutting fares, announced austerity measures (including a possible pay cut) and asked for cost-cutting suggestions. In four pages his paper showed why sacrifice is needed and asked for cooperation.

Story Idea No. 146

Sponsor employee Olympics
And feature the winners

Editor Scott McCarty, in his *Intercom* magazine, invites readers to go for the gold in a wide variety of fields—fastest typist, most languages, longest uninterrupted work attendance. It's a great idea, especially for slow summer months. And it just might earn some space in the local media.

Story Idea No. 147

Covering office decor
Offers a quick feature

Editor Marnie Johnstone carried a short article on making one's office one's own in *Rapport*, the newsletter for employees of Canada's Department of Consumer and Corporate Affairs. Her picture of an employee with a fish tank in his office showed just how far some people had gone. Get your photographer and make a quick tour of offices in your building. Get employees to talk about how and why they picked the decor they did.

Story Idea No. 148

Address the issue
Of work and family

Thierry Sagnier, editor of *Bank World*, recently covered family leave, child care, and phased retirement to make the point that flexible work arrangements raise productivity. Since so much is written in the media on this topic, finding the angle you want should be a snap; interesting statistics should be easy to come by. Carry a sidebar feature on what other companies are doing. This works especially well when you know your employer does more than anyone else locally. "Work and the family" is a hot topic. Editors who haven't taken up the subject yet should be starting their research.

Story Idea No. 149

Change your
Employees' language

When employees choose words badly it hurts the company and it can have legal repercussions. Editors Lisa Best and Don Johnson wrote an article that looked hard at everyday employee language in *US West Today*. They warned against using phrases such as "blowing 'em out of the water" and ended their story with a list of "competitive etiquette tips"—such as avoiding "warlike terms" and "words with conspiratorial overtones." This is a story every editor should consider running. For quotes, talk to your corporate attorney.

Story Idea No. 150

Features on kindergartners
Popular with employees

Editor Sharon Soltero devoted four pages of her publication to showing the latest crop of employee kids off to school for the first time. She edits *The Dispatcher*, a publication of the Nebraska Public Power District. This is a recurring feature that might not do much for the bottom line but, if eliminated, would lead to employee revolt. Other publications feature lists of employees' children when they graduate from college.

Story Idea No. 151

Suggest a "dump day," Then cover the event

Become known as an innovator. Work through channels to suggest to upper management ideas they may not have thought of. Make your publication proactive. Suggest a "dump day" to encourage employees to trash outdated reports, letters, and memos. Southwestern Bell held a series of these days and editor Jennifer Hopkins-Jackson covered them in *Telephone Times*. The program was aimed at reducing paperwork. When you implement your program, tie it in with a housecleaning of file cabinets.

Story Idea No. 152

Find individuality, Then feature it

Carbider editor Dick Henderson asked employees to send him their humorous and unusual personal memos. Along these same lines, you could ask for employees to share their unusual nicknames with you. Certainly there is individuality, self-expression, and a sense of style in the workplace—but don't expect these things to come out and bite you. You have to go and find them.

Story Idea No. 153

Provide employees a yardstick
To measure customer satisfaction

How do you measure the job your company is doing? Editor Korte Brueckmann does a good job of this in his *Utili Bits*, the employee monthly of Tacoma Public Utilities. He created a column entitled "Complaints & Compliments." The complaints about service during the quarter are listed under a tragedy mask. The compliments appear under the smiling mask of comedy. Brueckmann uses a similar approach in communicating the safety record.

Story Idea No. 154

Look outward, angel,
For cosmopolitan view

Most editors focus on company doings rather than on the marketplace. The result is an insular view of the world. Rich Palymay, editor of GE's *Aerospace News*, breaks out of this box with "Market Monitor," a half-page feature on the political and market forces that shape the company's future. Palymay's brief items paraphrase stories from newspapers and the aviation trade press. If employees understand economic and political influences that affect their employer, it helps both them and their organization. It tempers worker demands when times are tough.

Story Idea No. 155

Ask for story ideas
In this catchy way

Tired of asking for story ideas in the same old ways and getting the same meager results? Then follow the example of *Focus* editor Cam Buchan. Buchan splashed "Headline for rent" across the front page, above a section reserved for employee-submitted stories on customer service. He told readers of the London Life publication "*Focus* wants to hear about these stories—the good, the bad, and the ugly." The humorous approach struck just the right tone with readers.

Story Idea No. 156

It is never too late
For a purpose statement

It's never too late to create a statement of purpose for your publication. Julie Aho, editor of *Contact*, wrote an excellent statement of purpose : "*Contact* is published as an open and straightforward source of company information for active and retired employees of Minnesota Power." Don't just slip a new purpose statement into your publication or revise an existing one and expect readers to notice. Do a story on the purpose statement. Elaborate on what it means. Tell how it evolved, and what was considered for inclusion and then dropped, and why.

Story Idea No. 157

How to cover
Total quality

In the past, initiatives came from on high, and if you needed to find out what the corporation was doing, you called a VP. But in the age of total quality, changes come from below and the editor's problem is finding out what quality teams are up to. Joyce Miller, editor of Bethesda Hospital's *Quality Times*, includes an insert with brief updates on the teams, listing their goals, status, and results. Team members get recognition and the readers see the process at work.

Story Idea No. 158

Rescue those at sea
In alphabet soup

"I spent my first two months at the company floundering in a giant sea of alphabet soup," wrote an American Security Group employee in the publication *Wings*. Sean Neville's humorous story defines several dozen corporate acronyms. Make an annual update of company acronyms a feature of your publication. Have fun pointing out which acronyms are "in" and which ones are "out." There isn't a better way to improve organizational communication. You'll clear up many misconceptions: few employees will admit they don't know what an acronym stands for and fewer yet will ask.

Story Idea No. 159

Go beyond stories
About charity and volunteers

Many companies talk about their charitable efforts, but they rarely notice the social utility of the company's day to day business. The editor of *Continental Bulletin* knows that it pays to tell employees how their industry helps society just by doing its ordinary business. The editor asserts employees should feel good about working for an insurance company because it was pressure by the insurance industry on car makers that resulted in air bags being standard equipment on many autos. Without mentioning employee volunteers or charity, give readers at least one reason why they can be proud of working for your company.

Story Idea No. 160

Tap into employee ideas
Regarding safety issues

Many messages on safety reek of condescension. They often go unheeded. *Exxon Today* editor Mike Long avoided this problem by asking readers for their own solutions to safety problems. He used a graph to depict safety at the oil company. It revealed that most injuries occur between 9 and 10 a.m. and 2 and 3 p.m., and that December is the most dangerous month. Long then asked readers what the company should do and included a clip-out card for their comments. Here's another way to tackle safety: Find some recent accident victims willing to reveal what they did wrong and why. Ask them to write the stories for you, either with a byline or anonymously.

Story Idea No. 161

**Help your readers
Learn from mistakes**

Do you have the freedom to take a long, hard look at company failures? Editor Suzanne Dirksen has a feature called "Lessons From Losses" in *Eagle's Nest*, the employee publication of Guaranty National Co. It describes agents' costly mistakes and points out ways to avoid such situations in the future. Dirksen takes her bad examples from old claim files to preserve the privacy of agents.

Story Idea No. 162

**Here's a health feature
With a dramatic difference**

Rather than use national norms for weight, blood pressure, cholesterol count, etc., an insert in *Communicator Newsmagazine* lists the health statistics for American

Fidelity employees. Employees see how their health compares with that of co-workers, not with some remote, abstract statistic. Kudos to editor Brian Mauck for this innovative coverage. Most editors would have been satisfied with a photo or two of employees giving blood samples, and a few lines of copy.

Story No. 163

The time is right
For your column

Read what *Harper's Magazine* editor Lewis Lapham had to say on why he writes a long, personal column every issue: "An editor . . . is somebody who has something to say, and not merely a mechanic who assembles bits and pieces. An editor is a person with a point of view, opinions. The magazine is an opinionated form." If you don't have a column from the editor, maybe now is the time to reconsider.

Story Idea No. 164

Sell employees
On lateral moves

How do editors handle the touchy issue of upward mobility nowadays when the typical career graph is flatter than the

Siberian tundra? Marilyn Faludi of the New York Power Authority sells employees on other routes to career fulfillment in her publication, *Currents*. She shops the idea of lateral transfers as a good way to get ahead. Since this requires new thinking, the idea—a reality in most corporations today—does require selling. She points out that lateral transfers can prevent stagnation and add oomph to the resume. "It's clear there's little room to move up at Power Authority," declared one HR manager she interviewed. "So if people want to stay challenged, they've got to move around."

Story Idea No. 165

A reminder
About the obvious

Felix Bjorklund of IBM Europe offers this: "Employees should read about company news before it gets into the press." Sounds obvious. Is it? You should be on the distribution list for all corporate news releases. You should also work out an arrangement with your public relations people that ensures employees get the news before the public does. This could mean forsaking your regular publication for a bulletin board announcement or the public address system. It's okay if public relations handles this: decide who can get the news to employees the fastest—not whose job it is. Of course, most communicators have been on the distribution list for news releases since day one. Still, Bjorklund's comment would not have been noteworthy if there were not a problem.

Story Idea No. 166

The job of this magazine: Criticize the management

Is your publication making your company better? If not, it's time to try something new. That's what Allstate did. Editor Susan Addelson created that rarest of things—a corporate publication that criticizes management. It's called *Leaders*. Addelson writes from the point of view of management science experts. Her provocative managers' journal shows that top management has committed itself to change. *Leaders* reports on today's manager, someone who inspires empowered employees to try creative solutions and take risks. It takes readers (about 8,000, mostly front-line supervisors) outside Allstate, showing not what Allstate is doing, but how the corporate world is making itself more competitive and customer-oriented. It replaced another publication that had an inside focus. "We had to break managers out of the idea that 'this is the Allstate way of doing things,' " she said. The best time to introduce such a publication is on the heels of a change, when everyone's enthusiasm is greatest.

Story Idea No. 167

Illustrate the value
Of employee ideas

Bill Kress, editor of *USAir News*, borrowed a technique from United Way to show the dollar value of employee suggestions. He put a line drawing of an airplane in each issue. Each issue, as the suggestions piled up, a greater area of the airplane was darkened. The airplane represented a savings of 67 million dollars, and the 1,000 ideas submitted up to that point in the year were worth $36 million. The chart showed at a glance that employees and their ideas do make a difference.

Story Idea No. 168

Breathe life
Into an obit

Aetnaizer editor Louise Axelson wisely relied on a man's own words and thus avoided the dry, impersonal touch of too many obituaries. Her two-page piece about the death of a CEO contained plenty of candid quotes, including one from a sparring match with Ralph Nader. When Nader commented on the 'inordinate power' held by insurance executives, the exec retorted, "Well, you didn't exactly come here in a canoe yourself, you know." The real person—witty, self-confident and dynamic—came through.

Story Idea No. 169

Poll your readers
To defuse harmful language

A corporation cannot control which of its employees the media may target for attribution. It hopes the media speak to seasoned public relations people, but that isn't always the case. Barbara Bellemare, writing in *Insight,* the management newsletter from Syncrude Canada, reminds employees not to use loaded language when talking to the media. She provides less emotionally-charged synonyms for such words as "toxic," "sludge" and "tailings pond." Survey your readers for terms they use that sound provocative or controversial on the six o'clock news. Then print those terms, alongside the synonyms that lead to clear, calm thinking on explosive subjects.

Story Idea No. 170

Refine the art
Of small talk

"When it comes to social and business conversation," say Anne Baber and Lynne Waymon, "most of us act as though we're still at the eighth-grade dance." They offered some sensible tips in *Impact*, a publication of Nynex: remember names, ask intelligent follow-up questions, prepare a conversation agenda, be seriously curious, and learn to how to say goodbye. A useful and fun feature to do. The authors illustrated it with cartoons finely attuned to the subject.

Story Idea No. 171

Make corporate
Values stick

Betty Nelson, editor of *Intracorp News*, wanted to give permanent form to her company's newly-minted mission statement. She included a 3 x 5 inch sticky card printed with a synopsis of the message in her publication. Doing so enabled readers to remove the backing and stick the card on any flat surface in their office. Nelson reported that this special feature came in at under $1,000. One reservation: we wonder how much it will cost to remove the stickers once a new mission and values statement emerges.

Story Idea No. 172

Provide important facts
During staff reductions

How do you handle layoffs? Do laid-off employees imagine that they have been singled out as superfluous? To counteract such misconceptions, *US West Today* editors Lisa Best and Don Johnson provided readers with a detailed statistical breakdown of the latest firings. The focus was on laid-off managers. Readers discovered how many were getting the sack, where they came from, and the average salary and length of service. There was also a breakdown by sex and race, showing that the suffering was shared equally. This story faced unpleasant reality squarely. We all know that misery likes company; not so generally admitted is that misery also likes equality. No one wants to think he or she has been singled out to be fired.

Story Idea No. 173

Publicize corporate action
Taken to end fraud, theft

Cars have stickers in their windows warning that the vehicles are equipped with alarms. You can accomplish the same thing by detailing what your company is doing to stop fraud and theft. USAir admitted it was losing six million dollars a year in pilferage and fraud. To fight this, *USAir News* announced the introduction of a Hot Tip Line. The toll-free, 24-hour hotline is run by an outside firm: the third party should increase employees' confidence in the system's confidentiality. It would be wise to have statistics on how the thieves are taking money out of honest employees' pockets.

Story Idea No. 174

Here's an item to use
When you need a filler

Sometimes the hardest thing to come up with is a meaningful filler. A filler from Wisconsin Bell's *Trend Bulletin* pinpoints one of the curses of voice mail—the phone number uttered too quickly: "A reminder to slow down! For everyone who leaves a voice mail message, there is someone else who has to decipher it .... Speak into the receiver, speak slowly, and speak clearly—especially your name and phone number."

Story Idea No. 175

Help employees deal
With information overload

Information overload is a popular and necessary subject for employee publications. *Cap Gemini* ran interesting story titled "You Are What You Read." Editor Bruce Zewe polled a dozen or so employees on what they read, and how they managed the flood of information. *Computerworld* turned out to be the most widely-read publication, but the article showed that employees read a wide array of magazines, professional journals, and newspapers. To cope, consultants divide their reading into two piles: a top 20 percent of "important" publications, and all the rest. You could make this a lively article.

Story Idea No. 176

Getting a handle on all
Your bilingual employees

Bilingual employees are in increasing demand as companies try to improve service to customers who don't speak English. The *Communicator Newsmagazine,* from American Fidelity Group, contains a coupon for employees to fill out, asking what languages they speak fluently. Only one thing was missing—an incentive for employees to increase their work load by becoming interpreters. Speaking of bilingual employees, Editor Joe Mark Horn wrote "In Another Language" for *Visions,* from Atmos Energy. The article profiled customer service reps who deal with Hispanics as well as German-speaking Mennonites and Cajuns.

Story Idea No. 177

Get employees
To 'fess up

In a feature in *Southwestern Banker,* editor Michelle Gorel asked employees to finish the phrase, "Nobody would believe it if they knew that I . . . .". Two of several responses: "... am allergic to all 14 of my pets"; "... starred in an Ex-Lax commercial while in college." Another employee, inspired by a Lone Ranger episode, recalled an indiscretion of his youth—trying to rob a bank.

Story Idea No. 178

Use all the photos
That are fit to print

Editor Michelle Medley of the *Dallas Morning News* celebrated the 21st birthday of her employee magazine *Intercom* by going into the archives and returning with enough photos for a nine-page album of staff photos. Sounds reasonable when you realize she had 21 years of photos to select from. Most of the images were memorable; of course it helped that they were taken by professional photographers. A year-end wrap-up feature is an ideal time to highlight photos that have gone unused during the year.

Story Idea No. 179

A new way to write
Safety stories

Editors Joseph Fumo and Randi Kreger, writing in Johnson Controls' *Monitor,* interviewed managers from plants with the best safety records and then boiled down everything they were told into six basic safety tips. Then, using a bulleted format, they made the prescriptions much easier to digest and remember. By writing about safety ideas that work at Johnson Controls they created an immediacy that you just can't attain by quoting safety platitudes and national statistics.

Story Idea No. 180

Use quizzes to transplant
Ideas into readers' minds

Send a message to employees that it's time to become more culturally aware. Rather than even hint that their people may not have been "aware", editors Wayne Cousins and Cynthia Dyson provided a quiz for the readers of *People*, publication of BC Hydro. The quiz allowed employees to make that decision themselves. The quiz was on cultural diversity, and covered everything from the name of the knife carried by Sikhs to the definition of discrimination. Quizzes encourage readers to examine their own attitudes, rather than bashing them over the head with a message. The headline introducing the quiz asked, "Are you culturally aware?"

Story Idea No. 181

Colorful company symbols
Are meant to be revered

You never know what you'll find once you start digging through the archives. Consider writing about an old and beloved company symbol. Take, for instance, the "Phoebe Snow" story, which recently graced the pages of *Inside Track*, from Conrail. Once Phoebe was the famous symbol of the Lackawanna Line, one of Conrail's predecessor railroads. The delicate, white-painted engine made her run to Buffalo on the Lackawanna because the line's anthracite-fueled engines spewed less soot than the engines of other lines, which relied on soft coal for energy. Gary Fulton's piece made a great nostalgia story. Sometimes, as with Betty Crocker's picture, the company symbol has undergone periodic updating. It's fun to show your readers the many forms your corporate symbol has taken over the years.

Story Idea No. 182

A new way to write
A story of change

Why do people fear change so much, even after you have warned them and carefully explained the reasons for it? Even after all that you still encounter many who are hurt and angry once change happens. Editor Glenda Bartosh, writing in *MB Journal*, publication of MacMillan Bloedel Ltd., warned employees to prepare for powerful psychological reactions when faced with layoffs, restructurings, and plant closings. Bartosh, taking a cue from Elizabeth Kubler-Ross's work on mourning, told readers to expect to go through denial, anger, bargaining, depression, and acceptance. Why? Because change is a little like death. Mentioning those same steps in an article on change will help readers grasp they are not alone—many have gone before them.

Story Idea No. 183

Tell your readers
What you want

Be specific when you ask employees for story ideas. And don't ask for long essay-type answers. Send out a reply card, like Pat Hollenbaugh, editor of *The Missile,* from the naval Air Weapons Station in Point Mugu, California. Hollenbaugh never asks for an answer that can't fit on one line of the reply card. If she wants more she calls the employee. Matt Pozel, editor of *KC Focus,* includes a full-page form for employees' story suggestions. Submission categories include news items, awards, births, illnesses, etc. Pozel tells readers exactly what he wants.

Story Idea No. 184

Cover a plant's closing
With warmth, dignity

Many editors ignore the fact a company plant is closing, trying to avoid one of the most difficult jobs in writing—doing justice to an emotional event without falling into bathos. We salute *The Paper*'s "A Salute," a tribute to the employees who "walked off the plant site for the last time Aug. 31." The eight-page insert included many photos, and nostalgic sidebars consisting of short "remember when" facts ("Remember when the gates were locked from 3-4 p.m. and no one could leave early?").

Story Idea No. 185

Corporate ban on booze
Leads to tough talk

It's one thing for a company to declare a policy for public relations purposes and wink at violations of it. It's another to announce an unpopular policy and carry it out. Texas insurance company USAA recently forbade drinking during company-sponsored events. Editor Kathi Whitley communicated the news to employees in *Highlights*. She didn't mince words: "You are expected to arrive at a USAA party sober and not get around the policy by sneaking out to drink." If your company has announced a new policy, you owe it to your readers to find out how strictly it will be enforced and what punishment offenders will receive.

Story Idea No. 186

Make your fillers
Useful and interesting

Editor Dana Williams issued a warning: Photocopy faxes before you file them. Why? Because thermal fax paper is highly acidic. It can decay to the point of illegibility in only two years. What's more, the acid can migrate to other documents and destroy them. This item appeared in *Weekly*, the newsletter of Washington Water Power and it teaches three good lessons: (1) fillers make good copy, (2) readers read them, and (3) readers use many of them.

Story Idea No. 187

Running CEO's speech
Gets new message out

There are times to run a speech verbatim. The last approach seemed like the right move when the Bristol-Myers Squibb CEO announced a shift in corporate policy: "From now on, as we develop new products, raw materials will be weighed against each other for environmental impact. The ones most friendly to the environment will be chosen," noted CEO Richard Gelb, as reported in *Dotted Line*, from the Drackett division. If your CEO is articulate, it affords you the chance to run his or her speeches verbatim. When you do that, no one has an excuse for not getting the message.

Story Idea No. 188

Find a sales success story;
Spin an intriguing yarn

Written as a dramatic narrative, "Money on the Table," a feature in *Pulseline*, tells about two Occidental Insurance underwriters of Hawaii, Ltd., who realized that a Buddhist mission serving 10,000 people had an inadequate pension plan. The pension plan was managed by a competitor. The pair did their homework and presented their plan to 36 religious leaders scattered among five islands. When the plan was accepted, they hired a translator to call on Japanese clients. Sales success stories like this one make good reading and teach valuable lessons painlessly.

Story Idea No. 189

Give employees tips
Without preaching

You've seen them: pieces that quietly exhort workers to do a better job. Sometimes it's a message from the boss telling everyone to be more conscientious. Terri Hughes, managing editor of Albertson's *Today*, offers a section that accomplishes the same thing. It's called "Career Development." In it are small articles such as "How to Handle Angry Customers," and an exercise to develop "active listening." It's a nifty way of enlisting readers' interest by appealing to their self-interest.

Story Idea No. 190

Consider running
Book reviews

Have you read *Creating Demand* by Richard Ott? How about *Negotiating Rationally* by Max H. Baserman and Margaret A. Neale? If you haven't, you'd know about them if you read "Corporate Library News" in Saskatchewan Telecommunication's publication, *SasTel News*. Editor Jean Freeman not only reviews new business books, she prints photos of their covers. Even if your company doesn't have a corporate library, an occasional round-up of hot titles in business or employee relations brings new interest and prestige to your publication.

Story Idea No. 191

Guaranteed human interest:
The brand-new citizen

Employees who have just become U.S. citizens almost guarantee an interesting feature. Read this lead from a story in *Hydraulics Today*, a publication from Parker Hannifin, to discover the value in features like these: "Leonard DeSantiago, a machinist's specialist in our lab department, became a U.S. citizen on March 13. Leonard came to the United States in 1966 from Guadalajara, Mexico. The opportunity to vote was a primary reason for his decision to pursue citizenship. It took about one year from the day he filed his application to the day he became a citizen. Although no test was required, Leonard studies American history as a personal project." This sends a good message, wrapped inside an "employee spotlight" piece.

Story Idea No. 192

Mother's Day feature
From hell doesn't faze
This editor

Editor Carol P. Smith found the right way to do Mother's Day features. Last spring, *People's Energy News* ran its fourth annual Mother's Day feature. Smith made what could have been a mammoth, thankless chore easier by enforcing a few simple rules: Moms must be employees of the company—spouses were not acceptable because of limited space. Children could write about their mothers on an entry form provided in the announcement. Photos could only feature mothers with their children. Smith repeated the procedure for Father's Day. The results: upbeat, full-page features in May and June, with a minimum of headaches for editor Smith.

Story Idea No. 193

Is it a filler? Or Something bigger?

Editor Margaret McCormick of *Inside Farmland* ran a short piece on the seventeen cultures represented at her plant and seven languages spoken there. Sounds like it might make a big story about multiculturalism on the shop floor. But of course you'll never know until you determine exactly what the story (or filler) is at your company.

Story Idea No. 194

Foreign business story
Weaves in a little history

Which country, boasting a population that's growing at more than 8 million people a year, has 25 percent of the world's electric light sales? Answer: India. This interesting tidbit was found in a sidebar, "About India," in a story about GE international sales in *GE Lighting News*. Don't overlook the value of a history or geography lesson when writing about foreign business.

Story Idea No. 195

Reveal the secrets behind
Your great photograph

Interview your photographer. Find out how he or she got that great shot. If you don't, you could be losing half the value of an outstanding picture. "The Story Behind the Picture" appeared in *Pride*, a publication of Commercial Flight Systems Group. Editor Debra Austin interviewed her photographer, Guy Mancuso, who explained how he shot his photo. Mancuso took extra care that lights didn't bounce off the cockpit window and ruin his photo. The result was a classic picture of a confident-looking pilot, glancing over a smorgasbord of dials, lights, and switches. Outside the window, the runway stretched to the horizon.

Story Idea No. 196

Self-help stories tell readers Company cares about them

Eight ways to prevent cancer...interested? So were the readers of *Donnelly News,* no doubt. Editor Marilyn Matula includes several heavy doses of self-help information and health talk in every monthly issue. The same edition that carried the cancer prevention piece also featured a big spread on drunk driving, explaining that there are several types of drunk driving offenses in her state. Supported by telling statistics, this story suggests that the company cares about its employees.

Story Idea No. 197

Visiting employee's backyard Results in wildlife feature

Karen Hale, editor of *The Energizer*, publication of Transco Energy Company, had fun when she visited the backyard of employee Nerice Birney. That's because Birney turned her backyard into a wildlife habitat. Sure, it's just a feel-good story. But take time to smell the roses, editor—readers enjoy hearing about each other's lives outside of work. That's what they talk about over lunch, isn't it?

Story Idea No. 198

Pick an interesting business, Then show how you serve it

Provide your readers with a clear picture of your customer. Translate what employees do in terms they can appreciate. "Employees Help Customer Forge Expansion" put a recognizable face on a customer of PacifiCorp. Editor Nancy Varekamp assigned a human interest feature about Monte Paddleforth, owner of Eagle Bronze company, which casts realistic sculptures of Western characters. Remember, few people, especially people on the line, are inspired to do better work by seeing a balance sheet alone.

Story Idea No. 199

Visitors touring plant Offer feature material

Betty Steck, managing editor of *Boeing News*, combines obligatory photos of visitors touring the plant on one page and calls it "The Guest Book." First, it makes an interesting page; second, it demonstrates that people come through the facility regularly and that they are treated warmly. The reader sees Boeing representatives squiring around high school students, oldsters and Rotarians—this is good PR and a morale booster. If you know the visitors are suppliers or potential customers, it's productive to interview them for a story to accompany the photos.

Story Idea No. 200

Selectively chosen small items
Can be worth their weight in gold

Good fillers pay for the space they occupy ten times over. Here's an example: "Wisconsin Electric buys more than $15,000 worth of copy paper each month. Half of it never gets used before it's thrown away. That's because few employees use both sides of the paper." This is an info-byte item that appeared in *Currently* in a shaded box. Editor Anne Spaltholz runs a good number of small items in the publication. They lend a feeling of informality and intimacy to the layout.

Story Idea No. 201

Parent-to-parent tips
Could be standing feature

When the subject is day care, forget what the experts say. What do your employees say? After all, they're really the experts when it comes to the local situation. Editor Lynn Hannough ran a feature in *Rendez-Vous* on the topic of finding dependable day care. In addition to profiling several employees and their families, she created a sidebar of tips from those employees who'd been through the day care mill. Cover health from the standpoint of employee experience as a regular feature in your publication.

ABOUT THE AUTHOR:

Edward G. Bauer has more than 25 years of experience as an organizational communicator, writing and editing employee tabloids, magazines, newsletters, and customer publications for such firms as GT&E, Signode Corporation, Bankers Life & Casualty Company, Dartnell Corporation, and Nightingale-Conant Corporation.

He has also served as director of public relations for Dartnell and Nightingale-Conant. He founded two successful subscription newsletters, *Working Together* and *Successful Closing Techniques,* for Dartnell. Mr. Bauer has published more than 1,000 articles on such topics as management, customer service, telemarketing, interpersonal relations, and selling.

Currently he writes and edits *Creative Selling*, a subscription newsletter published by Economics Press of Fairfield, New Jersey. Upon graduation from the University of Illinois with a B.S. degree in journalism, he began his writing career as a reporter with the Decatur, Illinois *Herald & Review.*